## In The Wild

# Lynx

*Stephanie St. Pierre*

*Heinemann Library*
*Chicago, Illinois*

Designed by Depke Design
Printed in Hong Kong

05 04 03 02 01
10 9 8 7 6 5 4 3 2 1

**Library of Congress Cataloging-in-Publication Data**
St. Pierre, Stephanie.
   Lynx / by Stephanie St. Pierre.
      p. cm. -- (In the wild)
Includes bibliographical references (p.   ).
   ISBN 1-58810-109-6 (lib. bdg.)
   1. Lynx--Juvenile literature. [1. Lynx.]  I. Title. II. Series.
   QL737.C23 S714 2001
   599.75'36--dc21
                              00-012653

**Acknowledgments**
The author and publishers are grateful to the following for permission to reproduce copyright material:
Tom Brakefield/Corbis, pp. 4 (far left), 4 (far right), 8, 9, 15, 16, 17; Jeff Vanuga/Corbis, pp. 4 (center), 22; Terry Whittaker/Frank Lane Picture Agency/Corbis, p. 5; Doug Plmmer/PictureQuest, p. 6; Tim Fitzharris/PictureQuest, p. 7; Marcello Calandrini/Corbis, pp. 10, 23; Joe McDonald/Corbis, pp. 11, 20; Darrell Gulin/Corbis, p. 12; Dr. Robert Franz/Corbis, pp. 13, 19; John Warden/Index Stock, p. 14; W. Perry Conway/Corbis, pp. 18, 21.

Cover photograph: Dr. Robert Franz/Corbis

Every effort has been made to contact copyright holders of any material reproduced in this book. Any omissions will be rectified in subsequent printings if notice is given to the publisher.

Some words are shown in bold, **like this.** You can find out what they mean by looking in the glossary.

# Contents

# Lynx Relatives

There are several different kinds of lynx. This book is about the Canadian lynx. It is related to other cats like the bobcat, the caracal, and Siberian lynx.

Siberian lynx

caracal

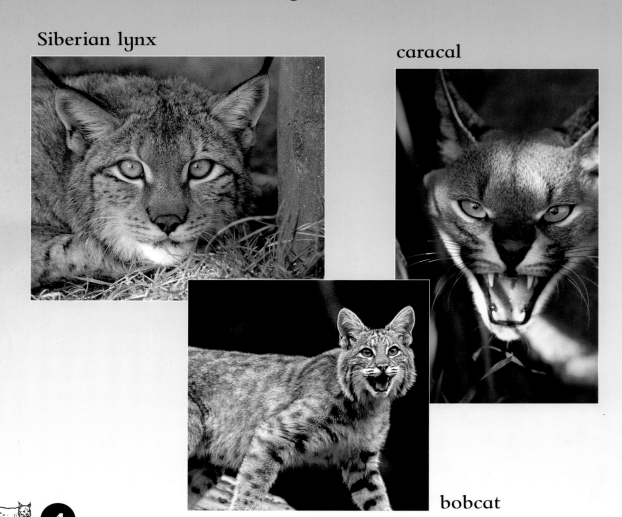

bobcat

All of these cats are wild. They are all related
to house cats, but they are bigger. A
Canadian lynx is about the same size as a
cocker spaniel.

# Where Lynx Live

The Canadian lynx lives in the northern part of North America, in Canada and Alaska. It is also sometimes found in the northern United States.

The lynx is a shy animal that usually stays far away from people. It likes forests and **woodlands** in the mountains.

# The Family

The lynx may live alone or with a few other lynx. Unlike many other cats, the lynx does not always want to be alone.

In very cold weather, lynx will take **shelter** inside caves, hollow trees, or logs. The lynx's fur gets very thick and long during the winter to keep it warm.

# Living in Snow

The lynx's fur is light gray with a few spots. This helps it hide in trees and snowy woods. Its tail is very short. A long tail would be too heavy to drag through deep snow.

The lynx's feet are very big. They have thick fur padding to help keep the lynx's paws warm. The lynx's big feet are like snowshoes.

# Climbing

Lynx are good climbers. They like to sit in tree branches and look around. This lynx has a good view of the woods.

The lynx may wait in a tree for **prey** to pass below. It jumps down onto the prey to make a quick **kill.**

# Hunting

The lynx sometimes hunts alone, but it also hunts with other lynx. A group of lynx may **stalk prey** and surround it. Then one lynx makes the **kill.**

If a larger animal, like a wolf, tries to take its kill, the lynx will run away. The wolf and the mountain lion are both enemies of the lynx.

# Eating

The lynx eats lots of different small mammals and birds. It will sometimes eat deer. Its favorite food is the snowshoe rabbit.

If there are not enough snowshoe rabbits for the lynx to hunt and eat, the lynx **population** will get smaller. Lynx will not have as many cubs as usual until there are more snowshoe rabbits again.

# Babies

Lynx cubs are born in the late winter or early spring. There are usually two to four cubs in a **litter.**

The cubs stay in a hidden **den** until they are a few months old. Then they come out to play and learn to hunt.

# Growing Up

Lynx are **nocturnal.** They spend most of the day sleeping. Young lynx go hunting with their mothers when the sun is coming up or in the evening.

When they are not learning to hunt, the cubs like to climb trees. Sometimes they go for a swim.

# Lynx Facts

- The lynx has very tall, pointed ears with long tufts of fur on them. These tufts help the lynx hear the softest sounds in the woods.

• Lynx are usually silent, but they can make growling and purring sounds. They cannot roar.

# Glossary

**den** safe, hidden living space
**kill** dead animal to be eaten
**litter** group of babies born at the same time
**nocturnal** active at night
**prey** animals hunted for food
**population** group of the same kind of animals all living in one place
**stalk** watching and carefully following
**shelter** place to keep safe and warm in

# Index

# More Books to Read

Barrett, Jalma. *Lynx*. Woodbridge, Conn.: Blackbirch Press, Inc., 1998.
An older reader can help you with this book.
Bonners, Susan. *Hunter in the Snow*. New York: Little Brown & Company, 1994.
Schneider, Jost W. *Lynx*. Minneapolis, Minn.: Lerner Publications Co., 1994. An older reader can help you with this book.